# There's a traffic cone stuck on my head!

Liam Midwood

# There's a traffic cone stuck on my head!

Copyright © 2009 Liam Midwood

The moral right of the author has been asserted.

Apart from any fair dealing for the purposes of research or private study, or criticism or review, as permitted under the Copyright, Designs and Patents Act 1988, this publication may only be reproduced, stored or transmitted, in any form or by any means, with the prior permission in writing of the publishers, or in the case of reprographic reproduction in accordance with the terms of licences issued by the Copyright Licensing Agency. Enquiries concerning reproduction outside those terms should be sent to the publishers.

Matador
9 De Montfort Mews
Leicester LE1 7FW, UK
Tel: (+44) 116 255 9311 / 9312
Email: books@troubador.co.uk
Web: www.troubador.co.uk/matador

ISBN 978-1848760-035

Typeset in 11pt Garamond by Troubador Publishing Ltd, Leicester, UK

**Matador** is an imprint of Troubador Publishing Ltd

*To Susan, Jake, Andrew and Danny, thank you for all your support and friendship over the years.*

# Contents

| | |
|---|---|
| **Rhyming Verse** | 9 |
| This book | 11 |
| Space | 12 |
| The animal explorer | 13 |
| A man called Guy | 14 |
| Bakery | 15 |
| Bathtime creatures | 16 |
| The cat, the rat and the dog | 17 |
| The Class Teacher | 18 |
| The effects of drink | 19 |
| The Penguin | 20 |
| The Queen's Dinner | 21 |
| The shopping list | 22 |
| Transport | 23 |
| Curry | 24 |
| The day dad fell in the toilet | 25 |
| In the park | 26 |
| There's a traffic cone stuck on my head | 27 |
| Pets | 28 |
| Types of pasta | 29 |
| Desserts | 30 |
| Magistos-incantem-restereo | 31 |
| Unlucky | 32 |
| What I would do to parents if I was Prime Minister | 33 |
| My stepmum is an evil witch | 34 |
| Types of biscuits | 35 |
| Topiary Terry | 36 |
| Mr Fantastic – our class teacher | 37 |
| Geoffrey, who followed fashion | 38 |
| Our teacher's hobbbies | 39 |
| Mr Brass, the Super Man | 40 |
| False identity | 41 |
| The Olympic Games | 42 |

| | |
|---|---|
| Ways to kill a wasp | 43 |
| The DIY expert | 44 |
| Airport | 45 |
| Farmyard meal | 46 |
| Jungle | 47 |
| The poet | 48 |
| Lunchtime | 49 |
| The shark | 50 |
| What to do | 51 |

**Limericks** — 53
Telly in Pwelli; The man from Wales; The man from Gwent; Cleaning; The mouse in the peas; The man and his bow; The man from Caerphilly; The man from Kent; The man from Stoke; The man from Cologne; The man from Trier; A man called Tony

**Miscellaneous Verse** — 59

| | |
|---|---|
| The four seasons | 61 |
| If you're in the Army | 62 |
| The Footballer | 63 |
| Light | 64 |
| What am I? | 65 |
| The arachnid | 65 |
| Sleepy Sloth | 66 |
| Formula One | 67 |
| Wee Willie Winkie | 68 |
| Mary had a little Lamb | 69 |
| Baa baa black sheep | 70 |
| Names of Refs at Bradford City | 71 |
| You're not going out like that, son | 72 |
| Rain | 73 |
| The swimming pool | 74 |
| | |
| What is Alström Syndrome? | 76 |
| Alström Syndrome UK | 77 |

# Rhyming Verse

## This book

Come on in and have a look
at the poems in this book.
There's no need to be afraid
of the poems I have made!
There's different poems for all sorts
of people who have different thoughts.
Haikus, Kennings and Limericks,
some are long and some are quick,
free verse and rhyming for different tastes
and a double acrostic of which you should be amazed.
I'll leave you alone and hope you enjoy
signed, yours truly, a poetic boy!

## Space

Black as coal,
dark as the night,
if you go into space
then do take a light.

The sun is in the centre
with planets around.
Asteroids and comets
these aren't the only things that can be found.

There's rockets and spaceships
and space stations as well.
When you land back on Earth
you'll have a story to tell.

Of meteors and rockets
the moon and the sun,
of when you were scared
and when you had fun.

So if you've got the nerve,
then get ready to go.
Fasten yourself in
spaceships don't move slow!

When you come Earthwards,
well what would you say,
about the time you spent
in the Milky Way?

## The animal explorer

Walk into the garden
what will you find?
A worm which is wriggling,
a mole which is blind?
Walk into the long grass
what is in there?
A grasshopper jumping,
a hedgehog or hare?
Look up to the sky,
what will you see?
A butterfly soaring
or a big bumblebee?
Walk into the woodland
and I will bet
that you will see a badger
prowling home to its sett.
Walk into the grassland
what can you hear?
The cloven-hoofed walk
of a red or roe deer.
Walk home at dusk
and look into the night
the tawny and screech owls
are all taking flight.
Now the mice are all resting,
the bats give a flap,
so it's time to go home now
and have a little nap!

# A man called Guy

There was a man named Guy,
who had a fondness for apple pie.
He had his dinner at eight,
and cleared his plate
and he was over seven feet high.

He staggered home drunk one night,
and gave his landlady a fright.
The TV was on the blink,
dishes were piled up in the sink
with his top hat, he turned off the light.

In the morning, when he arose,
he had a walking stick shoved up his nose.
He tugged it out,
then began to shout,
"Landlady where are my clothes?"

She told him they were right there,
at the foot of the stair.
He picked them up,
then dropped a cup,
and said, "That doesn't make a pair!"

She said "That is true,
one is red and the other is blue.
But when I folded them over,
a dog called Rover,
came in and ate quite a few."

# Bakery

"The bread needs slicing,
the fingers need icing,
the pasties need baking,
the jam tarts need making.
The biscuits need putting on the rack,
that buns not baked so put it back!
Put the customers orders in the bags,
this work must be done without any snags.
Put the drinks on the top shelf of the freezer,
the buns are baked, now add the malteser,
dear, dear this morning isn't going alright,
yes the bread is made brown, not white.
It's lunch put up the sign that says closed
that biscuits too hard so get it disposed.
You haven't sold a single pasty,
improve this afternoon or things will get nasty,
yes, put the butter and jam on the scone,
how will you cope when from this business I'm gone?"

# Bathtime creatures

In the bath there was a whale,
with a 20 foot long tail,
on the end was perched a snail,
its shell covered in detail.
But the shell of the snail
was held together with a nail,
which was terribly frail
and split revealing skin so pale
and so beautiful you could not fail
to follow the trail
of the exposed snail.
Meanwhile it crawled up the whale
the two creatures weren't to scale,
then there was heard a wail,
he'd accidentally swallowed the snail!

## The cat, the rat and the dog

The rats run away when the cats come close
for the sly old cat always knows,
that when he sees one in the street,
it's the dinner he would like to eat.
Now in a modern dynasty
somewhere in the Far West
they use the rats as cat catchers
and they are the best.
They put a rat in the doorway
and when the cat raises his head
he comes towards the cunning rat
and by a native is shot dead!
If it's the dog you want
to know the best about,
when a stray animal comes into the house
they will never let it go out.
This may sound a gruesome task
so I'll bring it to a close
by saying the common animal
gets a piercing through its nose!!

# The Class Teacher

"Straight backs please children,
and everyone look at me.
Susan, get down from the chair,
yes Kevin I know there's a bee.
David, I said sit up straight,
no, Stephen you can't watch the fish,
Kevin, don't sit on the table
and Stephen don't throw that dish!
David, I said sit up smartly,
Susan, don't put your pencil there.
Kevin, collect the rulers please
and Stephen don't stare.
I know we have a new man in class today,
his name is Mr Brooke.
He's going to read us some stories
from a well known book.
Yes Stephen, you may have heard it,
yes Kevin, I know you've heard it too.
I don't know if he'll read one story,
he may want to read a few.
Honestly, Mr Brookes" she said,
"They usually are quite quiet.
But when there's someone new in class,
they can make an almighty riot!"

# The effects of drink

You'll always feel frisky after drinking whisky,
you'll always feel loose after drinking orange juice,
you'll always feel free after drinking tea,
you'll always feel randy after drinking brandy,
you'll always feel fine after drinking lager and lime,
you'll always feel an outsider after drinking cider,
you'll always feel pale after drinking ale,
you'll always feel nice after drinking Smirnoff ice,
you'll always feel vain after drinking champagne,
you'll always feel merry after drinking sherry,
you'll always feel taut after drinking port,
you'll always feel thin after drinking gin,
you'll always feel fitter after drinking bitter,
you'll always feel dumb after drinking rum,
but even someone like the Queen
wouldn't think of drinking ovaltine!

# The Penguin

The penguin is one of the strangest
creatures that I know,
it doesn't live on warm dry land,
it lives on ice and snow.
The penguin has never flown
yet it has two wings,
nature will stop it flying about
and doing some other things.
For instance the penguin can't live on grass,
or pebbles or mountains or rocky sands,
but he can catch all the food he needs
he's the small bird who always stands!

## The Queen's Dinner

All different types of cuisine,
were served up to the Queen.
Chicken, fish and thick beef stew,
cabbage, carrots and mushrooms too.
She ate all the food politely,
holding her knife and fork lightly,
but when they brought the apple crumble,
with her fork and spoon she did fumble.
She put them down upon the plate,
and said "Oh that really is not great,
the smell of all this old seating,
would make anyone want to stop eating!"

# The shopping list

Apples, bananas and tins of peas,
coffee, bread and lumps of cheese.
Shampoo, cereal and a creamy dessert,
CD's, books and a brand new shirt.
Sausages and burgers for a barbecue tea,
and two new deodorants, one for dad, one for me.
Bags of potatoes and lots of cold meats,
and if I'm lucky, I might get some sweets!

# Transport

**Through the air**
A hovercraft flies very low
a hot air balloon flies very slow,
a helicopter can stay in one place
a rocket blasts off into space.
Concorde can fly very fastly,
but finally or lastly
is the common aeroplane,
everybody knows its name.

**At Sea**
Lifeboats help people in a disaster,
as ships come the yacht is the master,
sailing boats are the most well known
canoes can be rowed on your own,
tugs pull big boats out of the shore
and cruisers always leave you wanting more.

**Across the Land**
Cars trundle down the road,
lorries can hold a heavy load,
motorbikes whizz down the street,
when you're walking who will you meet?
On the back of every bus seat there's a bell,
there's one on bicycle handlebars as well.
Trains rattle down the track
but if you go you should come back!

# Curry

I had a chicken curry
and chips in two buns,
I think the curry was a good one,
because since I've had the runs!

I even ate the poppadom dip
though I didn't like the taste,
I didn't want to see
any food going to waste.

Then the chilli tickled,
when it reached the back of my throat,
if I'd have been in a restaurant
I would have been sick all down my coat.

But as it was,
it was just me,
I was at home,
so I threw up down the back of the settee.

I needed to use the bathroom
I needed to use it quick,
I lurched into the bathroom
and was violently sick.

But I think that chicken curry
really was sublime,
I'll have a curry next week
and get the runs, one more time.

## The day dad fell in the toilet

The day dad fell in the toilet
it really was very bizarre,
he went in looking quite normal,
but came out in the shape of a star!
He came out all covered in sewage
and up to his ankles in waste,
I said to him "When it comes to dress sense
you really have bad taste!"

## In the park

One day walking in the park,
I felt the need to have a fart,
it came out with such a stink
it made the old park keeper think.
"Who is that farting in my park?
They usually wait until its dark,
but this one is doing it by day
oh, I won't let him get away!"
It smelt of beans and curry sauce
the smell of it knocked out the horse.
It made mum's eyes water, the smell was so bad
then I remarked "Not in public dad!"

# There's a traffic cone stuck on my head

There's a traffic cone stuck on my head, mum
there's a traffic cone stuck on my head,
it means that I'm six inches longer
and can't fit into the bed.
She said "Lie down on the carpet"
and the front door immediately slammed.
I said "This cone is stuck on my head, mum
it really is completely jammed!"
She wriggled, tugged and twisted
until it was almost half off
then she dropped to her knees, gave out a sneeze
and then she began to cough.
I said "Mum what is happening
my head seems to be flattening I can almost feel my hair."
My mother just laughed and said "You are daft,
that's because there's no traffic cone there!"

## Pets

We've got a supply teacher today
'cos our teachers ill, away.
She brought it on herself you see
she said to form 8C
an almost suicidal line.
"Tomorrow bring your pets," so I brought mine.
Is a spider really a bad pet?
I've seen worse that you can get,
but when it climbed up our teachers back
she dropped to the floor with a heart attack!!!

## Types of pasta

Lasagne is a type of pasta
when made with béchamel sauce it's a disaster!
It should be made with mozzarella cheese
this is the way it is sure to please.
Ravioli and tortellini are filled with meat
macaroni is something I like to eat.
A fact that you may not know
is that farfalle is pasta in the shape of a bow.
Tagliatelle and linguine are very similar
they are like spaghetti only flatter.
The shape of penne and fusilli trap the sauce
pasta is a wonderful main course!

# Desserts

Sticky toffee pudding
is very, very sweet.
Strawberry cheesecake and ice cream
is something I love to eat.
Baked Alaska contains meringue,
as does lemon meringue pie.
Tiramisu is an Italian dessert
which I think you should try.
Christmas pudding is a dish
eaten at times of celebration,
bread and butter pudding is eaten
by an older generation.
Apple pie and chocolate mousse
can both be eaten with cream,
when you eat these desserts
you may think it's a dream!

## Magistos-incantem-restereo

First prepare your cauldron
and light a fire to put it on.
Put in a pigs gizzard and a newts spleen,
plus four pounds of plasticine.
Put in green and mouldy cheese
and six live rats riddled with fleas.
Add the snout of a warthog
and the eyeballs from your neighbours dog,
put in half a pint of slime
and boil it for a very long time.
Then add a lizard's skin
and leave it for a year in a rubbish bin.
Then pour in half a bottle of bleach
and a very old and battered peach,
now serve it up with blood and grease
and your magical powers it will increase!

## Unlucky

Last week I saw a black cat
crossed my path, just like that-
next day I had chicken pox.
The other week I knocked over the salt,
it wasn't really my fault,
next day I woke up with spots.
This week I walked under a ladder,
this made me feel even madder
next day……..
I had to go back to school!

# What I would do to parents if I was Prime Minister

I'd make them eat lumpy custard,
I'd make them do every test,
I'd make them stay in at lunchtime,
'cos I am the best!

I'd give them double homework,
I'd make them do P.E. in the rain,
I'd make them go to school on Saturdays,
and I'd bring back the cane!

I'd make them go to spelling class,
I'd make them eat school dinners,
when I am Prime Minister
us kids will be the winners!

## My stepmum is an evil witch

I know a different creature,
something from outer space
with her slime green teeth
and her gnarled and twisted face.

She rides upon her broomstick,
she wears a pointed hat,
she goes out in the dead of night
with her big black cat.

She has a long black cloak
which whispers on the ground
and with her magic wand
she curses everything around!

All her ghastly poisons
in a cauldron they shall brew
then she'll fly into bedroom windows
and poison me and you.

All the children run away
from her wide and evil grin,
when people knock upon her door
she greasily says "Come in".

But if you should step over the threshold
into her single darkened room
she shall raise her wand of destruction
and forthwith present your doom!

## Types of biscuits

Chocolate fingers are tasty and sweet,
Digestives are biscuits that I like to eat,
Wafer biscuits are rectangular and pink,
Rich tea break in half when put in a drink.
Hobnobs don't break when put in a cup
but left a long time they'll soak all your drink up!
Cream crackers are best when served with cheese
I can scoff 5 bourbon biscuits with ease.
Shortbread can be coated with caramel
to make millionaire shortbread you add chocolate as well.
Chocolate biscuits should not be put in a hot drink
'cos the chocolate will melt, and to the bottom sink.
I must now write about the jaffa cake
you make think its inclusion in this poem is a mistake,
it's a cake or that's what the name implies
and this is why people become mystified,
this will be discussed for a very long time
but now I've reached the end of my rhyme.

# Topiary Terry

There once was a young man called Terry
who was fantastic at topiary,
he cut all day long
but something went wrong
when he tried to carve into a ferry!

He tried to cut into the railing
and couldn't understand why he was failing.
"No matter how I
constantly try,
nothing will work", he kept wailing!

He tried to cut the sun, moon and stars
and an array of different cars
but nothing would work
because the silly old berk
tried to cut through thick metal bars!

He sat in his chair the next day,
the police took his tools away
he was all of a stew
thinking "What shall I do?
I'm irresponsible or that's what they say".

## Mr Fantastic- our class teacher

Our teachers a rocker!
Our teacher is cool!
Our teacher is the best
in the whole school!!!

He gives us all sweets
and he stands on his head,
if we try to do work
he sends us to the head!

He lets us play football,
he lets us run riot!
But when the head comes in
we go deathly quiet!

He asks us hard questions
and says that we're dim
when we don't know the answers
'cos we've not learnt anything!

He carries on in this fashion
till the head goes away
then he gives us all chocolate
and goes home for the day!!

## Geoffrey, who followed fashion

There was a man called Geoffrey Pratt,
who thought it fashionable that
when he was walking down the street,
his shoes almost fell off his feet.
He thought that he was really cool
but in fact he was a fool,
when walking past a big red bus
his shoe got caught in the wheel and thus,
the bus went speeding down the street
dragging Geoff along by his feet!
His head was battered on the floor
until it was painfully sore!
The bus came slowly to a stop
but, propelled by his flip flop
Geoffrey landed with his head
under a car and now he's dead!
The moral of this little verse
is to warn you of Geoffrey's curse,
don't follow fashion like all the rest
of your friends when getting dressed.
Don't buy the flip flops that you crave
unless you want an early grave!!!

## Our teacher's hobbies

Mr Johnson plays football in sandpits,
Mr Shaw imitates a giraffe,
Mr Lucas plays guitar with his teeth
and Mr Wright collects flies for a laugh!

Mr Alan takes ponies on holidays,
Mr Wilson reads books upside down,
Mr Edward uses knitting patterns
and Mr Wood runs naked through town!

Mr Ford plays cards with his reflection,
Mr Wells collects old violins,
Mr Burns always stands on his head
and Mr Smith used to think he had wings!

But the most ridiculous hobby,
the one which makes you stop dead,
with his binoculars, pen and paper
is our ornithological Head!

# Mr Brass, the Super Man

Our form teacher
Mr Brass
is the most boring person
in the class,
he writes long division
endlessly on the board
and sends us to the head
for any minor discord!
But in summer
when the kids are off school,
Mr Brass
becomes really cool!
He's a Super Man
or some may say,
when it's our school
holiday.
He dons new clothes
and flies away,
through the skies,
sunny or grey.
A Super Hero
saving us all!
But when the leaves
begin to fall
and all the kids
are back in class,
he's boring, stupid
Mr Brass!

## False identity

"Hello Mr Simon Mann,
I am from the news,
people from all over the country
have been expressing their views.

That your real name is Spider Man
is it really true?"
"Come in and have a cup of tea
and then I will tell you.

My friends all call me spider
'cos I climb trees, I know that,
I've a brother who hangs from ceilings,"
"So what do they call him?" "Bat".

"My parents call me Simon
so Simon is my name,
as for circulating rumours
you are the one to blame!

You've spread your thoughts like wildfire
all throughout the BBC,
there's someone out there called Spider Man
but it's definitely not me!"

# The Olympic Games

Every four years the Olympics come around
it's where all the top athletes can be found,
and this is something I have to say
about the sports that they play.

Archers, hold their bow and arrow ready
shooters, cock their guns and hold them steady,
in front of them they can see
the bull's-eye which may bring them victory!

Boxers, in their corners ready for a fight
at the Beijing Olympics which are on late at night,
in wrestling and judo there's a lot that's the same,
speed and throws, in both, are the aim.

In squash you hit a ball with a racket
in table tennis it must bounce before you can whack it!
In tennis they try to win match, set and game
in badminton the players try to do the same.

I didn't write about hockey or football
because I didn't have time to mention them all,
there will be lots more sports played in Beijing
and people will watch everything.

## Ways to kill a wasp

You can burn 'em with a laser,
suffocate 'em in your blazer,
you can shoot 'em with a gun,
or keep 'em to scare your mum,
you can roast 'em on a fire,
or scorch 'em with a magnifier.
You could use acid to burn 'em,
or put 'em in a lathe and turn 'em,
mash 'em like a potater,
kill 'em with a cheese grater,
you can drop 'em from a plane
or flush 'em down the drain.
You can splatter 'em, batter 'em,
shatter 'em or clatter 'em,
or find something else to do
when the wasps come bothering you!

## The DIY expert

When I've had my little nap,
I'll design a work of wonder,
something that is fancy
and can survive the rain and thunder!

Once I've had my little sleep,
I'll make a vast creation,
something intricately carved
that will sell in every nation!

Once I've had me 40 winks
I'll go out in the yard,
but then I'll have to have a kip
'cos a builder's life is hard.

I'll maybe cut a bit of wood
or paint a little bit,
but when I get up from me chair
that'll just be it.

I'll have to sit back down again
and have a little rest
so that I can make things
to my very best!

# Airport

When we leave the house
and get to the airport
we find out that we haven't got
everything we'd thought.

My passports on the table
my umbrellas in the hall,
my sister left her diary
and my brother left it all.

I'll grab a pack of polos
and a lemon barley sweet,
I'll also take some chewing gum
to stick to the airport seat.

My dad takes his cricket set
and a card for scoring
my brother takes his headphones
in case he finds it really boring.

He also takes his action men
piled up like the dead,
and a bucket of cold water
to tip over the pilots head!

We pack the car properly
making sure we've got everything,
there's just one small problem now
none of us can get in!

## Farmyard meal

When our sheep died
I said "Hurray,
we can have lamb chops
for dinner today!"

When our pig died
I said "Yippee,
we can have sausage sandwiches
for our tea!"

When our hen died
I said "Oh, great,
we can have roast chicken
on our plate!"

When our cat died
mum said to me
"Quickly run down
to the KFC!"

## Jungle

When you're in Tanzania
then you'll be filled with fear
and overcome with fright,
but what can you do
when elephant poo
fills up your car overnight?!

## The poet

The writer of this poem
is handsome, tall and slim,
well that's what this poem says
and it was written by him!

# Lunchtime

Should you be so kind
as to go and find
for your dog, some meat,
you'll have to be meaner
to the evil hyena
who fancies a nice canine treat!

# The shark

If in waters deep and dark,
you come across a hungry shark,
the only advice I can say
is that you must swim away!

## What to do

When you really don't know what to do,
when you really do not have a clue,
when you can't make a start,
think, where goes the interesting part?
Then you will need to think things through.

# Limericks

## Telly in Pwelli

There once was a man from Pwelli,
who watched football on the telly,
he drank cans of beer
and when no-one was there
he ate crisps and rested them on his belly!


## The man from Wales

There was a man from Wales
who fell onto the train rails,
he was taken to Cornwall,
where nobody at all
believed his extraordinary tales!


## The man from Gwent

There was an old man from Gwent,
who went on holiday in a tent,
but when night came,
it flooded, what a shame!
So back home he went.

## Cleaning

There once was a young man from Chard,
who thought that cleaning was hard,
so he paid a large bill,
every day, at free will,
to a lady called Mrs Mullard!

## The mouse in the peas

There was a man from Dumfries,
who bought a packet of peas,
he took it back to his house
but inside was a mouse
which he got out with a sneeze!

## The man and his bow

There was a man from Dunlow,
who bought himself a very nice bow,
he left it out in the night
and then got a fright,
in the morning it was covered in snow!

## The man from Caerphilly

There once was a young man called Billy
who came from Caerphilly,
he thought for a laugh
he'd go and swim in the Taff,
he froze for it was too chilly!


## The man from Kent

There once was a young man from Kent,
whose legs were extremely bent,
his house was too small
for him to live in at all,
so he had to live in a tent!


## The man from Stoke

There once was an old man from Stoke,
who drank copious cans of coke,
one day in bed,
thoughts went round his head,
he stopped drinking for the fear he might choke.

## The man from Cologne

There was a young man from Cologne,
who spent all his time on the phone
but he met with despair
when he fell down the stair
and broke every single bone.

## The man from Trier

There once was a young man from Trier
who had an extraordinary fear
that he'd have too much to drink
and in a river, sink
because of his passion for beer!

## A man called Tony

There once was a young man called Tony,
who was very tall, thin and bony,
so he became a cook
but he ran out of luck
when he choked on his own macaroni!

# Miscellaneous Verse

# The four seasons

## Spring

Crocuses growing
the first flowers in springtime
colourful and bright.

## Summer

Children on the beach
play under a sunlit sky
with buckets and spades.

## Autumn

Leaves fall from the trees
get carried under people's feet
as rain starts to fall.

## Winter

All the trees are bare
as snow falls and fires glow
all is dead or white.

# If you're in the Army

If you're in the Army, shoot,
if you find a shoot, eat it,
if you find eat, turn down central 'eating,
if you find Down, leave Northern Ireland,
if you find Ireland, swim to shore,
if you're sure, join the Army,
if you're in the Army, shoot.

# The Footballer

Attackblocker
Playmaker

Passpicker
Penaltytaker

Freekickbender
Cornerswinger

Shotstopper
Joybringer

# Light

Darkness breaker,
light receiver,
tear bringer,
sleep reliever,
thought shower,
object that spies,
what am I?
The eyes.

## What am I?

Branch bender,
paper lifter,
heat cooler,
leaf shifter,
door slammer,
rope swinger,
face gnawer,
chime ringer,
what am I?

Answer: The wind

## The arachnid

Scream provoker
thread spinner,
fly catcher,
hairy legged
cobweb maker,
skin tickling
arachnid.
What am I?

Answer: A spider

# Sleepy Sloth

Sleepy
Lazy
On a branch forever
Tired
Holding on.

## Formula One

From the starting grid, they set ofF
On the great track, at Monte CarlO
Racing in their various type of caR
Measuring up the other driver forM
Unbelievably…beating the SuberU
Lewis Hamilton, favourite of us alL
And they wait.. in the winners areA

One of them is in the Alpha RomeO
Not going too well, not going to wiN
Everybody knows that.. it is so truE

# Wee Willie Winkie

Wee Willie Winkie
runs through the town
upstairs and downstairs
in his nightgown.
He sometimes runs slowly,
he sometimes runs quick
and when the police catch him
they'll bang him in the nick!

## Mary had a little lamb

Mary had a little lamb
she said she'd call it Paul,
but she sold it at the fair
when it peed up the garden wall!


## Rub a dub dub
Rub a dub dub
three men in a pub
and what do you think they'll drink?
A lager, a shandy and a bottle of brandy
then to the floor they'll rapidly sink!


## I'm a little slug
I'm a little slug, short and stout
when you see me why do you shout?
I only eat leaves and lie about
why are you getting those slug pellets out?


## Twinkle, twinkle brand new bar
Twinkle, twinkle brand new bar
how I wonder where you are,
with tables from wall to wall
brilliant for our first pub crawl!
Twinkle, twinkle brand new bar
how I wonder where you are.

## Baa baa black sheep

Baa baa black sheep
why are you looking so glum?
"Well the sheep shearer shaved
all the wool off me bum!"


## Old Mother Hubbard

Old Mother Hubbard
went to the cupboard
and found out that it was bare.
This didn't please 'er
so she bought a fridge freezer
and put all the food in there!


## Round and round the garden

Round and round the garden
playing hide and seek
"Have you found me yet?
I've been here for almost a week!"


## Dr Foster

Dr Foster went to Gloucester
in a shower of rain,
he slipped on spilt rum
and landed on his bum
which still gives him terrible pain.

# Names of Refs at Bradford City

Mr Brad Fordhater
O. Pless
Dai Abolical
U. Sless
Ron Grules
A. Bysmal
A. Trocious
A. Palling
Mr Lostus the Game
Mr R. Sole
King No Idea of Rules

## You're not going out like that, son

You're not going out like that son,
you're not going out like that,
with your:
dyed black hair,
your nose ring,
your tattooed arms
and all that bling.
You've borrowed your dads old t-shirt
and his jewellery,
do you want to bring shame
upon our family?
Honestly, I can't believe it
you look a disaster,
it's the school parents evening tonight
and you are the Headmaster!

# Rain

Rain glistening on each leaf,
drops slide slowly down the window pane
as an endless torrent of water
gushes from the sky, as black as night.
The rain brings life to flowers
but lifelessness to cities,
as people stay inside
glancing occasionally at the window
to see if the downpour has ended.
As the rain slows and finally stops,
the sun breaks through low woolly clouds
clearing away the puddles that were left behind,
as though preparing for a new outburst.

# The swimming pool

Gliding gracefully through the water
with backstroke, breaststroke or crawl,
swimming underneath the surface
like a fish, before coming up for air.
Children whoop with pleasure
as they slither down the long slide
and splash into the water at its end.
Underneath showers falling powerfully
from taps set high above in the ceiling
as bubbles break through the surface.
A whirlpool powers people around
in ever-tightening circles
with bubble jets pushing them onward
around this circular paradise!
A Jacuzzi foams away silently
as people absorb the warmth
of its deep waters
and reflect upon the joys of swimming.

# What is Alström Syndrome?

Alström Syndrome is a very rare genetic disorder which may cause heart failure, progressive blindness from childhood, hearing loss, diabetes, kidney failure and liver dysfunction as well as associated problems. The symptoms arise at different stages making diagnosis difficult.

Heart failure (due to dilated cardiomyopathy) occurs in 60% of patients and often in the first few weeks of life. Rapid eye movements (nystagmus) and extreme sensitivity to light are also often early signs. Obesity is common in all children despite attempts to monitor diet. Type two diabetes often develops during puberty. The gene ALMS1 which causes this devastating, life threatening disorder has now been discovered.

# Alström Syndrome UK

Alström Syndrome UK (AS UK) is a registered charity set up in 1998 to provide support for families, professionals and carers affected by Alström Syndrome.

AS UK has been instrumental in developing specialised Alström Syndrome medical screening clinics for those affected. Here families get advice on the best treatments available to help maintain a good quality of life and delay progression on the disorder. Each year a number of combined multi-disciplinary clinics are organised- one alongside our annual family conference. Our annual family conference gives families a chance to hear talks from specialists on how best to mange the disorder and meet others affected. For our latest information visit www.alstrom.org.uk

Contributions of support and donations are gratefully received in order that the charity may continue to provide information and advice alongside developing research into the best treatments. We also welcome contact from patients and their relatives.

Tel 01803 524238
www.alstrom.org.uk
Registered Charity Number 1071196